Yo-Yo Ma

by Mary Olmstead

Chicago, Illinois

© 2006 Raintree
Published by Raintree, a division of Reed Elsevier, Inc.
Chicago, Illinois
Customer Service: 888-363-4266
Visit our website at www.raintreelibrary.com

Printed and bound in China by South China Printing Comapny.
10 09 08 07 06
10 9 8 7 6 5 4 3 2 1

Library of Congress Cataloging-in-Publication Data:
Olmstead, Mary.
  Yo-Yo Ma / Mary Olmstead.
      p. cm. -- (Asian-American biographies)
  Includes bibliographical references (p.   ) and index.
  ISBN 1-4109-1058-X (hbk.) -- ISBN 1-4109-1127-6 (pbk.)
  1. Ma, Yo-Yo, 1955---Juvenile literature. 2.
Violoncellists--Biography--Juvenile literature. I. Title. II. Series.
  ML3930.M11O46 2005
  787.4'092--dc22

                              2005005635

Acknowledgments
The publisher would like to thank the following for permission to reproduce photographs:
Alamy Images pp. 4 (Waring Abbott), 40 (Ambient Images Inc.), 33 (Image Gap), 38 (Black Star); AP pp. 35 (Wide
World Photos/Itsuo Inouye), 52 (WideWorld Photos), 57 (WideWorld Photos), 58 (WideWorld Photos); Corbis pp. 11
(Robert Holmes), 16 (Charles E. Rotkin), 24 (Bob Krist), 28 (Bob Krist), 31 (Bettmann), 36 (Bettmann), 43
(Bettmann), 44 (Bill Ross), 51 (Reuters), 55 (Neal Preston); Getty Images pp. 7 (Photodisc), 13 (Hulton Archive), 19
(Time Life Pictures), 20 (Hulton Archive), 22 (Time Life Pictures), 29 (Hulton Archive/Leo Vais), 49 (Carlo Allegri);
Granger Collection p. 15; Superstock p. 8; University of Pennsylvania Archives p. 46 (Allen J. Winigrad)

Cover photograph: Corbis (William Coupon)

Some words are shown in bold, **like this**. You can find out what
they mean by looking in the glossary.

Contents

Yo-Yo Ma is one of the world's greatest cello players.

Introduction

Yo-Yo Ma has been playing the cello since he was a young boy. He gave his first concert at the age of five. Because of his talent, hard work, and creativity, today Yo-Yo Ma is one of the world's finest cello players.

Yo-Yo Ma rocks his cello from side to side. He draws the **bow** across its strings. He concentrates completely. He seldom looks to see where to place his fingers. He throws his head back. His eyes close, his glasses reflecting the bright lights of the stage. His face is a mirror of the music he draws out of his instrument. During these moments Yo-Yo Ma feels at one with the music, with the other musicians, and with his audience.

Listening to Yo-Yo Ma play the cello in concert is magical. He springs onto the stage with youthful energy. He greets the audience and the **orchestra** with a warm smile. Taking up his cello, he cradles the large instrument in his arms. The audience grows quiet. Soon they are drawn into a story he tells using his cello.

Yo-Yo Ma loves making connections—to other kinds of music, to history, and to people. That is why his music appeals to so many different kinds of audiences. People like his sunny personality as much as they like his great talent. He travels the world bringing music and joy to people's hearts.

The Cello

The cello (also known as a violoncello) was invented in the 1500s. The cello is a four-stringed instrument, closely related to the violin. Cellos are about twice as large as violins. Their size makes the sound a cello produces much deeper than a violin's sound. For centuries cellos came in a variety of sizes. Since the 1700s cellos have been around four feet tall.

Cello players sit holding the instrument between their knees. The cello is balanced on a metal spike. They draw a **bow** across the strings of the instrument to produce a sound. At first cellos were only played as part of an **orchestra**. Today, they are played both as an important part of the orchestra and other musical groups, and as a **solo** instrument.

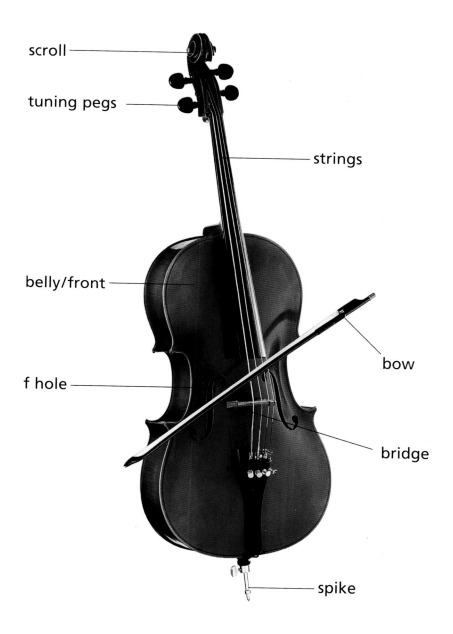

scroll

tuning pegs

strings

belly/front

f hole

bow

bridge

spike

The bow is drawn across the strings of a cello to produce the sound.

Yo-Yo Ma was born in Paris, the capital of France.

Chapter 1:
Early Childhood

Yo-Yo Ma was born to Chinese parents in Paris, France, on October 7, 1955. His father Dr. Hiao-Tsiun (hee-ow-shun) Ma was a violinist and music professor. His mother Marina was a singer. Yo-Yo has a sister who is four years older named Yeou-Cheng (yo-chung). The words "Yo" and "Yeou" both mean "friendship" in Chinese.

Yo-Yo's father studied at the University of Paris Conservatory of Music. For many years he worked at low-paying jobs until he finished his education. Times were hard for the young family. They lived in a one-room apartment with no heat. The first winter of Yo-Yo's life was very hard. His parents worried about their children living in such a cold room. Somehow, though, they made it through the winter.

Surrounded by Music

Yo-Yo was surrounded by music as an infant. Singing, playing, and listening to music was as natural as breathing for the Ma family. His mother had been trained as an opera singer. She sang in a beautiful, strong voice. His father played the violin. His sister played piano and violin. His parents played records of **classical music** for their children.

Yo-Yo's parents helped their son develop his musical talent. When he was very young, Yo-Yo could sing in tune. Yo-Yo began piano and violin lessons when he was three. His piano teacher was amazed at how quickly he learned. Dr. Ma taught his son to play the violin. He noticed that Yo-Yo did not seem very interested in it.

A Little Out of Tune

A family story says that when Yo-Yo was three years old he listened to his sister perform a piece of music on the piano. After she played Yeou-Cheng asked her little brother if she had played well. According to their mother, Yo-Yo hesitated before he spoke. He did not want to hurt his sister's feelings. "You played very well. You were great. But ... " Yo-Yo paused before he told her gently that she was a little out of tune.

The Sorbonne is a famous university in Paris.

A Big Instrument

One day Yo-Yo's father took him to the Paris Conservatory of Music. In the corner was a large double bass. It is a stringed instrument that is about twice the size of a cello. The double bass is so big that some adults stand up to play it. Yo-Yo stopped and looked at the huge instrument. He pointed to it and said excitedly, "That's what I want to play!"

Yo-Yo told his father he did not like the sound the violin makes. "I want a big instrument," the three-year-old said. The double bass was way too big for such a little boy, so Dr. Ma got Yo-Yo a small cello instead.

Years later Yo-Yo offered another reason why the violin did not hold his interest. He said his sister Yeou-Cheng was "a fantastic musician, and I probably thought I could never play as well."

Note by Note

Dr. Ma was Yo-Yo's first cello teacher. He had a special way of teaching. He did not start with easy pieces of music. Instead he taught Yo-Yo how to play music by one of the world's greatest **composers**, Johann Sebastian Bach. Bach wrote long, difficult pieces of **classical music**.

Johann Sebastian Bach (1685–1750)

The composer Johann Sebastian Bach was born in Eisenach, Germany. His parents died when he was about ten years old, and he was raised by his older brother. Bach held many musical jobs. He was a singer, musician, and music director. He married twice and fathered twenty children.

Bach was famous as a master of many instruments, including harpsichord, violin, and especially organ. A harpsichord is a stringed instrument that looks like a piano. Bach composed during the baroque period. It was a time in which many new musical forms and styles were developed. He wrote thousands of compositions, many for use in churches. He invented a new style of music for the harpsichord called the harpsichord concerto. Some of his great works include the *Brandenburg Concertos*, *Well-Tempered Clavier*, and the *Mass in B Minor*.

Short Lessons

The method Dr. Ma used to teach his son was simple. He gave very short lessons. Each day Yo-Yo only had to learn two measures of music. A measure is a few notes of music. Several measures make up a longer piece of music. Dr. Ma insisted that Yo-Yo learn each measure perfectly. That meant Yo-Yo had to memorize the notes. Then he had to practice them over and over.

Every day Yo-Yo would learn two more measures of a Bach **suite**, a long piece of music. Soon he learned to recognize patterns in Bach's music. Yo-Yo liked learning longer pieces of music this way, because he did not have to practice very long. After he learned every measure, he put them all together. He played beautiful, complex pieces of music.

Many young cello players find it difficult to memorize music. Yo-Yo explained why his father's method made it easy. "When a problem is complex, you become tense," he said. "But when you break it down…you can approach each element without stress."

Dr. Ma said Yo-Yo played "like a shining star." He had a good memory, and he concentrated better than most children his age. By the time he was five, Yo-Yo could play three Bach suites by heart. That year, he gave his first public **recital** at the University of Paris.

This is a page from a Bach manuscript.

The Ma family moved from Paris to New York in the early 1960s.

Chapter 2:
A Rare Talent

In 1962 the Ma family visited Yo-Yo's uncle in the United States. During their visit Yo-Yo and Yeou-Cheng performed at the Chinese-American Society in New York City. A man from the Trent School was in the audience. He was very impressed with the children's talent. He knew that Dr. Ma had taught them. After the **recital** he offered Dr. Ma a job as music director for the small private school. He wanted Dr. Ma to establish a children's **orchestra**.

Dr. Ma accepted. He had dreamed for a long time of starting a children's orchestra. The Ma family bought a house in the little town of Ormesson, not far from Paris. This way they could move to the United States and return to France each summer.

A Great Success

In the fall the family moved to New York City. Yo-Yo and his sister could speak French and Chinese but not English. They learned

English in school, but continued to study Chinese at home. Yo-Yo attended the Trent School, where his father taught. Fortunately for Yo-Yo, classes were taught in French as well as English.

In New York Yo-Yo and his sister played for great musicians. They played for **cellist** Pablo Casals. They played for violinist Isaac Stern. Stern had heard Yo-Yo play in Paris when Yo-Yo was five. He thought Yo-Yo was one of the best musical talents to come along in years.

Yo-Yo was seven years old when he was introduced to Pablo Casals. The little boy charmed the great cellist. Yo-Yo's playing impressed Casals. He wanted others to hear him play. Casals told a famous **orchestra conductor** named Leonard Bernstein about Yo-Yo. Bernstein included Yo-Yo on a television program called "The American Pageant of the Arts." The show was a great success.

Yo-Yo and Yeou-Cheng were invited to play with Pablo Casals at a benefit concert for the Kennedy Center in Washington, D.C. That night, November 29, 1962, the Ma children played in front of many famous people. President Kennedy and his wife Jacqueline were in the audience. The next day the *Washington Post* newspaper praised the musical ability of Yo-Yo and his sister. The praise made Yo-Yo want to work even harder to master the cello.

The Spanish cellist Pablo Casals encouraged Yo-Yo Ma's talent after the young musician played for him in New York City.

An Eager Pupil

When Yo-Yo was seven, he studied cello with a Hungarian cellist named János Scholz. Scholz was astonished. He watched as Yo-Yo learned with incredible speed. "He was so eager to acquire musical knowledge," Scholz recalled, "that he just lapped it up." Within two years Yo-Yo was ready to study with another teacher.

Famous violin player Isaac Stern (left) was one of many great musicians who spotted Yo-Yo Ma's talent.

Isaac Stern, the violin player, introduced Yo-Yo to his friend Leonard Rose. Rose was a cello player and a music professor at Juilliard. Juilliard is a famous school where many talented musicians have studied. Yo-Yo was very shy when he first met Rose. He barely spoke above a whisper in front of his new teacher.

At first Yo-Yo tried to hide behind his cello. He was awed by the wonderful sounds his new teacher drew from the instrument. Rose saw how shy his young student was. He tried to make Yo-Yo feel at ease. He told jokes and said silly things. Yo-Yo could not help but grin at his teacher's sense of humor. Slowly he began to feel more comfortable around Rose.

Eight Years With Rose

Rose liked his young pupil. He was amazed at his ability. Yo-Yo could memorize long and difficult pieces of music. He played with intense concentration. By the time he was twelve, Yo-Yo had learned some of the most difficult pieces of music written for the cello.

Rose told Yo-Yo to become "one" with his instrument. By this he meant that Yo-Yo should feel as though the instrument were a part of his body. Yo-Yo remembers Rose telling him, "The strings are your voice, and the cello your lungs." Yo-Yo was Rose's student for eight years. He remembers Rose as more than a teacher. To Yo-Yo, Rose was a good friend.

Leonard Rose taught Yo-Yo Ma for many years.

Leonard Rose (1918–1984)

Leonard Rose was a great teacher and musician. Like Yo-Yo Ma, he learned to play cello from his father.

Rose joined the NBC **Symphony Orchestra** when he was only eighteen years old. He played under the direction of famed **conductor** Toscanini. In 1939 Rose became **principal cellist** with the Cleveland Symphony. Four years later he became principal cellist with the New York Philharmonic. In 1946 Rose became a professor of music at Juilliard. He left the **orchestra** and devoted himself to teaching, playing cello **solos**, and making recordings. The many albums he made became classics of cello music.

It was during this period of his life that Rose worked with Yo-Yo Ma. Rose's playing was described as having a beautiful sound that was like a "ribbon of spun gold." A cello scholarship fund in Rose's name was set up at Juilliard after he died in 1984 at the age of 66.

Like Yo-Yo, many children start learning the cello at an early age.

Chapter 3:
Being Different

Yo-Yo knew that he was different from other American kids his age. He had been born in France to Chinese parents. He had learned to speak French and Chinese when he was very young. Yo-Yo was already a world-class musician on an instrument most children his age had never heard of. Being different was sometimes hard for Yo-Yo.

Other Talents

When they had lived in France, Dr. Ma taught Yo-Yo and Yeou-Cheng French and Chinese calligraphy. Calligraphy is a type of artistic handwriting. Dr. Ma taught these subjects the same way he taught music. He broke lessons into short parts. He worked hard to teach his children. He spent two hours planning a Chinese lesson that took only ten minutes for his children to do. Yo-Yo and Yeou-Cheng learned two characters (like letters) of Chinese a day.

Dr. Ma did not want his children to forget the languages they had learned when they were very young. When Yo-Yo and his sister grew a little older, they kept journals in Chinese. They also memorized short paragraphs in French each morning before going to school.

Yo-Yo described his father as someone who had a real gift for teaching children. He set high standards. He expected good work. The little steps his father built into the lessons helped his children learn easily and well.

Yo-Yo's parents were an important influence on him. They believed it was more important for Yo-Yo to be a good person than to be a good musician.

In His Own Words
My Parents

My parents taught me to believe in the soul,
in that something extra, in the beauty that
is in human nature.

From a poem Yo-Yo Ma wrote as a child

Chinese calligraphy is an artistic type of writing. It is often used to decorate paintings.

At Home

Dr. Ma was very strict. Home was a place to study and practice music. Yo-Yo and Yeou-Cheng were only allowed to have friends over to play music. Yo-Yo's mother taught her children to be kind. She raised them to be generous and caring. She taught them to have a positive outlook on life. Marina enjoyed her son's curiosity. When Yo-Yo asked a thoughtful question, she praised him.

Yo-Yo and his sister followed a daily schedule set by their parents. They were up by six each morning. Yo-Yo practiced the cello for half an hour before breakfast. He had to come right home after school to practice some more. Afterwards he did two or three hours of homework.

Dinner was at seven. After dinner the children could watch one hour of television. Bedtime was at ten o'clock. When he was twelve, Yo-Yo could stay up an extra hour. He often used that time to practice the cello.

Yo-Yo's parents took their children to Chinese movies to learn Chinese culture. Yo-Yo and Yeou-Cheng learned that the Chinese place more importance on the entire family as a whole than on just one person. They learned that hard work brought honor to the family. They learned that children shamed the family when they disobeyed or were lazy.

Dr. Ma encouraged Yo-Yo to learn about Chinese culture. This dragon is an important part of the Chinese New Year celebrations.

At home the Ma family spoke Chinese. Yo-Yo and Yeou-Cheng had to behave according to Chinese custom. They were supposed to work hard and obey their parents without question. They were not allowed to talk back.

Extra Pressures

Yo-Yo considered himself to be more American than Chinese. He wanted to be more like other kids he knew. Sometimes Yo-Yo and Yeou-Chung told their parents they had to use the library just so they could get out of the house and watch other people.

At school Yo-Yo often disobeyed his teachers. Once day, he was sent to the office. The principal told Yo-Yo that people expected more of him than they did of other boys his age. "You were not born to be like others," he told him. He said Yo-Yo was born to share his musical gift with the world.

Yo-Yo was bored at school. His abilities were far beyond his grade level. He began skipping school when he was in the fifth grade. He would take long walks or go to the park. Sometimes he went to the movies. In 1968 Yo-Yo began attending the Professional Children's School. The school combined the study of regular classes, such as math, English, and history, with classes in music, dance, or drama.

When Yo-Yo was bored with school in New York City, he would sometimes skip class and take a walk in the park to watch people.

Juilliard School

The Juilliard School was founded in 1905 as the Institute of Musical Art. In 1926 the institute merged with the Juilliard Graduate School and became The Juilliard School of Music. In 1951 the school added dance classes, and in 1968 theater classes. In 1969 the school changed its name to The Juilliard School to reflect that it was no longer just a music school.

The school is located in New York City and is thought to be one of the best colleges for training performers. Many famous performers such as actor Robin Williams and **composer** Philip Glass are graduates of the school. The school offers Saturday classes for advanced students aged eight to eighteen, as well as evening classes for adult students.

The high point of Yo-Yo's week was Saturday music lessons at Juilliard. Even there he sometimes skipped classes. He liked to sit in the cafeteria and watch people. Being around people who were just hanging out was something new to Yo-Yo. He was used to people who were always working. Yo-Yo loved going to Juilliard because he was curious about what other people were like.

Many famous musicians studied at the Juilliard School, including Yo-Yo Ma.

A Path to Follow

Slowly Yo-Yo began to realize he was very good compared to other cello players at Juilliard. It took him a long time to accept that others really liked his work. Yo-Yo played in the **orchestra** with a boy named Danny Phillips. Danny said that Yo-Yo was shy. "He didn't say a word when we first began to play together," he remembered. Yo-Yo was afraid people might like him only for his talent.

New Audiences

When Yo-Yo was thirteen, his family visited his mother's sister in Berkeley, California. Yo-Yo was invited to play with the San Francisco Little **Symphony**. His performance earned him new fans. The local newspaper wrote about him. Yo-Yo was described as someone whose talent placed him in the same company as the grand cello masters. He was compared to his teacher Leonard Rose and the great Pablo Casals.

Yo-Yo's cello playing was only part of the reason audiences loved him. Yo-Yo was charming and drew people to him. The Ma's knew their son had a promising future because of his great musical talent. They also knew that his talent could prevent him from having a normal childhood. That is why they limited his public appearances.

Disobeying

Yo-Yo was forbidden to do anything that might hurt his hands. Once, a friend asked Yo-Yo to go fishing with him. Dr. Ma said no. He knew a fishhook could injure his son's hands. Yo-Yo was disappointed. He knew he should obey his father, but he really wanted to fish. He found a way around the forbidden activity. His friend offered to bait the hook for Yo-Yo. That way, Yo-Yo would not risk hurting his hands. Yo-Yo agreed. It would not be the last time he did something his father disapproved of.

More than 130 young cellists performed at the same time in this concert in Tokyo.

Yo-Yo Ma in his late teens.

Chapter 4:
Growing Up

Yo-Yo's teachers thought he skipped classes because he was bored. They placed him in a special program so he could graduate early. When he was only fifteen, Yo-Yo graduated from high school. That summer he attended Meadowmount, a music camp for string instrument players. It was a summer Yo-Yo would always remember. The camp was far away from home in the Adirondack Mountains of New York State.

Yo-Yo had never been away from home with so many kids his age. His shyness melted away. Yo-Yo did his best to be "one of the guys." He wanted to fit in. He concentrated more on having fun than on his music. He did things he had never done. He left his cello outside in all kinds of weather. He missed **rehearsals**. He got caught painting graffiti on a wall.

Carnegie Music Hall in New York City is one of the many famous places where Yo-Yo Ma performed.

When Yo-Yo returned home in the fall, he had a new look and a new attitude. He wore a black leather jacket. He used swear words when he was not around his parents. Yo-Yo thought that his new clothes and new vocabulary made him seem more grown up.

Leonard Rose accepted his pupil's new look. He ignored the new vocabulary. Rose decided it was time for Yo-Yo to take his music a step further. He gave his young student a gift. He gave him the freedom to work on a piece of music with no suggestions from him. Rose encouraged Yo-Yo to experiment with different ways of playing. That year Yo-Yo gave his first **recital** at Carnegie Music Hall. He also met a piano player named Emanuel "Manny" Ax.

Leonard Rose knew Manny. He told Manny that Yo-Yo was an outstanding student. He encouraged him to go hear Yo-Yo play. Manny found Yo-Yo's cello playing to be unforgettable. A few months later Yo-Yo and Manny ran into each other in the cafeteria at Juilliard. They began playing music together. Slowly they became good friends. They continue to be friends and work together today.

What To Do Next

Yo-Yo was out of high school. He did not know what to do next. Yeou-Chang had moved away from home and was in college studying to become a doctor. Yo-Yo decided to visit her.

Yo-Yo and Yeou-Cheng spent time together. The visit made Yo-Yo realize that he was too young to move away to college. He signed up for classes at Columbia University in New York City so he could live at home. But Yo-Yo was not ready to do college work. He dropped out after a few months, but he didn't tell his parents.

Columbia University is in New York City. Yo-Yo Ma signed up for classes here after graduating from high school.

A Bad Decision

During the day, Yo-Yo practiced music at Juilliard. He wanted to be accepted there by other kids his age. He began drinking alcohol, even sometimes during **rehearsals**.

One afternoon, Yo-Yo was supposed to be at a rehearsal with the Children's **Orchestra** his father directed. They were preparing for a big concert. A few of the children in the orchestra were very young—only four years old. At fifteen, Yo-Yo was one of the older musicians. His father depended on Yo-Yo to help lead the younger children. But Yo-Yo never showed up.

Yo-Yo had been at Juilliard. He drank so much alcohol that afternoon that he passed out. Some teachers found him. They did not know he had been drinking. They worried he had overdosed on drugs. Yo-Yo was rushed to the emergency room at the hospital. When he woke up his mother was there.

Yo-Yo knew that he had shamed his family. He had worried his mother. He had let down his father and the entire orchestra by his absence. He felt terrible.

Shaping Up

The next summer was important for Yo-Yo in many ways. He performed at the Marlboro Music Festival in Vermont. It was the first of many summers Yo-Yo spent there. He played in an **orchestra** under the direction of Pablo Casals. The great **cellist** was now 95 years old. Yo-Yo was inspired by the commitment Casals and the other musicians made to music.

That summer at Marlboro, Yo-Yo became friends with Jill Horner. They had met briefly a few months earlier. They ran into each other again at Marlboro and began spending time together. By the end of their stay, Yo-Yo told Jill he thought he had fallen in love with her. At first, Jill was amused. Yo-Yo was younger than she was. She thought of him more like a little brother. They went for bicycle rides and talked. They got to know each other better.

When he was seventeen, Yo-Yo decided he was ready to get a college education. He could easily have made his living being a full-time musician, but he wanted to be a well-rounded person. There were things other than music he wanted to learn. He enrolled at Harvard University in Cambridge, Massachusetts. Jill Horner left to spend her junior year of college in Paris. The two kept in touch with letters and phone calls.

Young musicians attend the Marlboro College, Vermont, to study with famous musicians, like Pablo Casals, shown here conducting.

Marlboro Music Festival

Marlboro, Vermont, is home to a world-famous center for advanced music studies called Marlboro Music. The center plays an important role in the development of **chamber music** in the United States. For seven weeks each summer, master concert artists work with young musicians who show great talent. They play together in chamber **ensembles**. The experience of working with older, professional musicians offers young artists a chance to improve their skills and learn from the best. When he was a teen Yo-Yo Ma spent several summers at Marlboro. He **rehearsed** and performed with great musicians, like Pablo Casals.

Harvard University in Cambridge, Massachusetts, is one of America's top colleges.

Harvard

One of the most important things Yo-Yo learned in college was how to learn. He had been far ahead of other students when he was growing up. He had not had to work very hard. In college a whole new world opened up to the young musician. Yo-Yo took classes in history, **anthropology**, literature, and the natural sciences.

In anthropology, Yo-Yo learned about the Bushmen. They are a tribe of hunter-gatherers who live in the Kalahari Desert in Africa. Many years later the class inspired Yo-Yo to explore musical traditions in Africa and other countries.

Yo-Yo formed a trio with two other music students. He gave **solo** concerts at Harvard and in other cities. He was becoming more famous. Requests for him to play poured in from around the world. It was hard to keep up with his studies. Yo-Yo thought about dropping out, but his father insisted that he stay in school. Yo-Yo and his father decided he would limit himself to one concert a month during the school year.

This picture shows Yo-Yo Ma performing in Philadelphia in 1982.

Chapter 5:
A Rich, Full Life

Yo-Yo Ma and Jill Horner went to different colleges, but they kept in touch with letters and phone calls. They saw each other whenever they could. Ma wrote many letters to Horner. In them he said things he was too shy to say in person. Horner began to take him more seriously. They wrote each other every day and spent long hours on the telephone.

In 1978, at the age of 22, Ma and Horner got married. At first, his parents did not like that Ma had married someone who was not Chinese. They worried he would forget his Chinese roots. However, after a while, they accepted Ma's choice. The young couple lived near Boston. Jill taught German at Harvard University. Yo-Yo was **artist-in-residence** there.

An Operation

In 1980 Ma had an operation to correct a problem with his spine. Ma's spine curved too much. Years of cello playing had made it worse. Ma knew that the operation carried a risk of nerve damage that might affect his fingers. If he did not recover fully, he might not play the cello again. He and Horner talked about the operation. They were prepared for whatever happened.

After the operation, Ma wore an upper-body cast for six months. While he recovered from the operation, Ma thought about his life. He thought about what held meaning for him. He questioned his decision to be a musician. He worried that he was not a regular person with a normal life. He began to wonder what life would be like if he could not play the cello anymore. The operation was successful and Ma realized how happy he was to be a **cellist**.

Starting a Family

When Ma and Horner decided to have children they wanted to make sure the children would know about both their Chinese and American backgrounds. They gave their two children both Chinese and English names. Their son Nicholas (Ping-Chou) was born in 1983. Their daughter Emily (Ping-Lan) was born two years later.

Yo-Yo Ma and Jill Horner married in 1978.

Ma was very busy with his music. He played up to 150 concerts a year. Sometimes he was gone for two or three weeks at a time. He came home very tired from his trips. A few days later, he would have to leave again. It was a hard schedule for him and his family to get used to.

In order to make sure he could be a good father to his children, Ma limited his concert schedule. He did not perform at all during the month of July. He also refused to perform on his children's birthdays.

A Cellist's Life

For fifteen years after he graduated from college, Ma led the life of a successful **classical musician**. He received invitations to play with famous **conductors** all over the world. He recorded music. He continued to perform with his friend Manny Ax. They were both willing to try many possible ways of playing a piece of music. They worked well together and people liked their music.

Honoring His Parents

Ma became famous, but he still remembered his Chinese upbringing. Chinese culture teaches people to respect the wisdom that comes with age and experience. Ma still turned to his parents for their opinions. By asking his parents what they thought about his music, Ma showed his respect for them.

Yo-Yo Ma and Manny Ax met through Ma's cello teacher, Leonard Rose, when they were teenagers.

Ma trusted his parents because they were honest with him. Ma remembered an expression his father once used to describe his playing as a very young child. He had said little Yo-Yo could "make his **bow** sing." Ma continued to work hard to keep the song in his bow.

These musicians playing with Yo-Yo Ma are playing traditional instruments during a performance for the Silk Road Project.

Chapter 6:
Exploring Other Worlds

In the 1990s, Ma began to step outside his music world. He thought about the **anthropology** class he had taken at Harvard. He remembered watching films shown in class about the Bushmen. They lived in the Kalahari Desert of Africa. Ma wanted to learn about their music. In 1993 he went to Africa.

The visit made a lasting impression on Ma. He listened to old men play instruments made of everyday materials. They used sticks, bones, and old cans. He watched the trance dance. It is an ancient dance in which villagers sing, dance, and clap. Sometimes they dance for hours, until someone falls down. That person is thought to have special powers. Ma made a film about his experience.

Reaching New Audiences

Ma soon became involved in a television series called *Inspired by Bach*. Each program in the series featured one of Bach's cello **suites**. Bach wrote these six long pieces of music just for the cello. Each television show paired Ma with a different artist.

For the first suite, Ma and a **landscape designer** created a public garden in downtown Toronto, Canada. They filmed the different steps involved in building a public garden. Yo-Yo played a Bach cello suite in the background. For the other programs, Ma teamed up with an architect, two **choreographers**, an actor, and ice skaters.

Ma had fun trying something new. He liked the idea of playing Bach for a different type of audience. He was proud of the beautiful garden he helped to create in Toronto.

Working with Children

In the late 1980s, Yo-Yo appeared on children's television. He was a guest on *Sesame Street* and on *Mister Rogers' Neighborhood*. Sometimes his young son Nicholas appeared with him. In 1999 Ma appeared on children's television again. He appeared as a cartoon character in the cartoon series *Arthur*. His character was a giant floppy-eared rabbit who wears glasses and carries a cello. Ma said that working with children was among the things he was proudest of having done.

Bobby McFerrin introduced Ma to a new type of music.

Ma wanted young people to be open to **classical music**. By appearing on TV Ma thought children would come to appreciate this type of music.

Different Kinds of Music

Ma began learning to play other kinds of music. He recorded *Hush* in 1992 with singer Bobby McFerrin. McFerrin introduced Ma to **improvised** music. Ma continued to learn new things from other musicians. Mark O'Connor and Edgar Meyer taught him how to play Appalachian **folk music**.

The three musicians made an album in 1996 called *Appalachia Waltz*. Several years later, they teamed up again to record *Appalachian Journey*. It won a Grammy Award in 2000 for Best Classical Crossover Album.

Silk Road Project

In 1998 Ma began the Silk Road Project. The Silk Road Project looked at the music, the art, and the history of different countries along an ancient trade route from China to Europe. Ma gathered musicians from the United States and from countries that lie on the ancient trade route–China, Mongolia, Iran, Uzbekistan, Tajikistan, and Azerbaijan. They wrote new musical works for the project. Much of the new music mixed the instruments and musical styles of the different countries.

The project linked its work to the work of other groups and museums. A two-year series of festivals was planned. Ma and a music group called the Silk Road **Ensemble** traveled across the United States, Canada, Europe, and Asia. The biggest festival was the Smithsonian Institution's Folklife Festival on the Mall in Washington, D.C. in the summer of 2002. Around 400 musicians, artists, and others from modern-day Silk Road cultures took part.

Edgar Meyer (left) and Mark O'Connor taught Ma how to play Appalachian folk music.

In 2001 Yo-Yo Ma was presented with the National Medal of Arts by President George W. Bush.

Marco Polo and the Silk Road

Yo-Yo Ma's Silk Road Project was named after the Silk Road, an ancient trade route named for the silk that was carried from Asia to Europe. During the 1200s people knew very little about East Asia. A merchant named Marco Polo traveled the ancient route and began bringing products from Asia to Europe.

C-100

In 1990 Ma helped form the Committee of 100 (C-100), a group of Chinese-Americans who are leaders in their fields. C-100 is a non-profit organization devoted to issues concerning the Chinese-American community.

An Ambassador

Through his many projects, Yo-Yo Ma has become one of the few **classical musicians** known outside the world of music. His great talent and warm personality have made him an ambassador for the world of classical music to the rest of the world. Through Ma many people have come to learn about and appreciate music.

Glossary

anthropology study of human beings and their cultures

artist-in-residence person who lives on the campus of a college or other institution. In exchange for a salary and living arrangements, the artist performs and sometimes teaches classes or gives lectures

bow wooden stick with horsehairs stretched from end to end. The bow is used to play a stringed instrument, such as a cello or violin.

cellist person who plays the cello

chamber music music played by a small group of people intended to be heard in a small space

classical music music in the formal, European tradition

composer person who writes music

conductor person who directs or leads an orchestra or other musical group

choreographer person who directs the movements of dancers

ensemble small musical group

folk music traditional, popular music of a culture or people

improvised music that is created on the spot and not written down

landscape designer person who plans and designs gardens

orchestra group of musicians playing together. Orchestras always have string instruments, such as violins and cellos.

principal leading performer. The principal cellist is the leading cello player in an orchestra.

recital concert given by an individual musician or students to show their skills

rehearsal practice for a musical performance

solo individual performance

suite piece of music that contains several different sections

symphony long and complex song played by an orchestra

symphony orchestra large orchestra of winds, strings, and percussion instruments

Timeline

1955   Ma is born on October 7th in Paris, France.

1959   Ma begins playing cello.

1960   Ma plays in his first public performance at Paris University.

1962   Ma family moves to New York City.

1971   Ma graduates at 15 from the Professional Children's School in New York.
       Ma plays a recital at Carnegie Hall in New York.

1976   Ma graduates from Harvard University.

1978   Ma marries Jill Horner.

1980   Ma has surgery on his spine.

1983   Ma's son, Nicholas, is born.

1985   Ma's daughter, Emily, is born.

1990   Ma helps to establish the Committee of 100.

1998   The television series *Inspired by Bach*, with Yo-Yo Ma airs.

2000   *Appalachian Journey* wins a Grammy Award.

2001   Ma is awarded the National Medal of the Arts.

Further Information

Further Reading

Ashley, Susan. *Yo-Yo Ma*. Milwaukee, Wis.: World Almanac Library, 2004.

Chippendale, Lisa A. *Yo-Yo Ma: A Cello Superstar Brings Music to the World*. Berkeley Heights, NJ: Enslow Publishers, 2004.

Ma, Marina and John A. Rallo. *My Son, Yo-Yo*. Hong Kong: Chinese University Press, 1995.

Addresses

Committee of 100
677 Fifth Avenue
3rd Floor
New York, NY 10022

ICM Artists
40 W. 57th St.
New York, NY 10019

Juilliard School
60 Lincoln Center Plaza
New York, NY 10023

Arthur M. Sackler Gallery
Smithsonian Institution
P.O. Box 37012
Washington, D.C. 20013

Index